Hen

by Ann K

AXIS education

Acknowledgements

Cover design: Oliver Heath, Rafters Design

Illustrations on pages 5, 7, 11, 15, 17, 19, 23, 25, 27, 29, 33, 35, 37 and 39 © Paul Gardiner, 2005. The right of Paul Gardiner to be identified as the illustrator of this work has been asserted by him in accordance with the Copyright, Design and Patents Act, 1988.

Brinsford books are a direct result of the findings of a two-year authoring/research project with young offenders at HMYOI Brinsford, near Wolverhampton. Grateful thanks go to all the young people who participated so enthusiastically in the project and to Judy Jackson and Brian Eccleshall of Dudley College of Technology.

First published in Great Britain by Axis Education Ltd

ISBN 1-84618-001-5

Axis Education PO Box 459
Shrewsbury SY4 4WZ

Email: enquiries@axiseducation.co.uk

www.axiseducation.co.uk

Sharon had her hen night at the disco.

She wore her new dress.

It was red and gold.

Kim wanted one but they had sold out.

Sharon and her mates went in the big limo.

There was drink in the limo

and fab music.

They sang and drank.

Tower Hamlets	
Suppliers Code	AVA
Price	£4.95
Invoice Date	01/11/2006
LOC	CUB
Class	428.6
Barcode	C001277884

There was a box in the limo.
It was like a desk with no legs.

Kim said there could be more drink in there.
Jo said it could be drugs.

They asked the man what was in it.

"Do not open it," said the man.

"It has my stuff in it."

They came to the disco.

It was a fab night.

Sharon got drunk.

It was late.

It was time to go home.

They got back into the limo.

The man stopped the limo.

He had to go to the toilet.

"Open the box," said Kim.

"We can have a giggle."

The lid went up.

There was a man in the box.

He was folded up in there.

He was dead.

Kim gave a yell.

"Oh, God," she said.

"He is dead."

The man was green.

He stank of rot.

"I cannot stand this," said Kim.

"Shut the box," said Sharon.

"Do not let the man see.

He told us not to open it.

Shut it."

But the man in the box sat up.

"No, no," yelled Sharon.

"Shut the lid."

"Not me," said Kim.

"Nor me," said the rest of them.

"I want to get out," said Sharon.

But they could not get out.

The limo was locked.

Green stuff slid off the man in the box.

There were scabs all over his face.

The stink was bad.

"I will be sick," said Jo.

Then the green man put out his hand.

His fingers tapped on the limo floor.

"No!" yelled Jo.

But the green hand went on to her hand.

Jo saw her hand go green.

It was like a sped up film.

First her hand, then a leg.

They began to drip green stuff.

"Help me," yelled Jo.

Kim went to batter the glass where the man sat in front.

It would not shatter.

At last it broke.

She got into the man's seat.

She got out of the limo.

Sharon went to get out but the green man was there.

Jo went to get out but the green man was there.

"Help us," they yelled.

Kim ran.

It was dark. There were no lights.

It was wet.

She had left her mobile in the limo.

She fell in the mud.

There was no one to help.

Her dress was black with filth.

Splash! She was in a puddle.

"Help, oh, help!" she sobbed.

But there was no one in the dark.

At last she saw a glint of light.

It was a phone box.

Now she could call for help.

She went into the phone box.

Someone had smashed it.

She could not call the police.

"I want to go home," she sobbed.

Where was she?

She did not know.

And she had to help her mates.

Then there was a light.

She saw it from a long way.

It was a car.

She ran to it.

Then she had to stop and think.

It could be the limo.

She hid by a wall
in the dark.
If it was the limo
she did not want them to see her.

The car came by.

It was not the limo.

It was not the man from the limo.

She ran to stop the car.

"Help, help," she said.

"I want to call the police.

Do you have a mobile?"

"What is the matter?" said the man.
"Tell me and I can help."
Kim told him about the limo
and the green man.

"You have had a lot to drink," said the man.
Kim had to make him see.
She told him more.

"I am not drunk," she said.

"We must find the limo and my mates."

Then he said he would take her to the police.

Kim got into the car.

Now she could get the police.

But would her mates be okay?

It was hot in the car.

There was an odd smell.

Kim had smelled it before.

"I do not like this," said Kim.

"Let me out!"

But she could not get out.

The car was locked.

There was a box in the car.

A box like a desk with no legs.

Something hung out of the box.

It was red and gold.

It was a bit of a dress.

The dress Sharon had on for her hen night.

Glossary

broke	having no money
dark	not light
green	the colour of grass
mates	friends
mobile	mobile telephone
music	sound made by instruments or singing
phone	short for telephone
room	part of a building separated by walls, floors and ceilings